W9-AEU-707

CLIMATE CRISIS

Plants and Insects

Stephen Aitken

Cavendish Square

New York

Published in 2014 by Cavendish Square Publishing, LLC
303 Park Avenue South, Suite 1247, New York, NY 10010

Copyright © 2014 by Cavendish Square Publishing, LLC

First Edition

Website: cavendishsq.com

This publication represents the opinions and views of the author based on his or her personal experience, knowledge, and research. The information in this book serves as a general guide only. The author and publisher have used their best efforts in preparing this book and disclaim liability rising directly or indirectly from the use and application of this book.

CPSIA Compliance Information: Batch #WS13CSQ

All websites were available and accurate when this book was sent to press.

Library of Congress Cataloging-in-Publication Data
Aitken, Stephen, 1953–
Plants and insects / Stephen Aitken.
    p. cm. — (Climate crisis)
Includes bibliographical references and index.
Summary: "Provides comprehensive information on climate change and its effects on plants and insects"—Provided by publisher.
ISBN 978-1-60870-462-0 (hardcover)
ISBN 978-1-62712-042-5 (paperback)
ISBN 978-1-60870-633-4 (ebook)
1. Plants—Juvenile literature. 2. Insects—Juvenile literature. 3. Climatic changes—Juvenile literature. I. Title.
II. Series.
QK49.A35 2013
581.7'22—dc23
2011012967

Editors: Megan Comerford/Joyce Stanton/Christine Florie
Art Director: Anahid Hamparian
Series Designer: Nancy Sabato

Photo research by Laurie Platt Winfrey, Carousel Research, Inc.

Cover: Alamy / PhotoAlto

The photographs in this book are used by permission and through the courtesy of:
Alamy: Bob Gibbons, Titlepage + 38, 40-41; Blickwinkel, 6; Jack Thomas, 33; Malcolm Schuyl, 34-35; Juniors Bildarchiv, 39; Tao Images Limited, 44; Jeff Greenberg, 46-47. *Cutcaster*: Background details. *Getty Images*: Michael Durham/ *Minden Pictures*, 4; Ashley Cooper/Visuals Unlimited, 28-29. Minden Pictures: Mitsuhiko Imamori, 27. *Superstock*: Indexstock, 8-9; Mark Newman, 21; AGEfotostock, 22-23.

Printed in the United States of America

Contents

Introduction

Plants come in all shapes, colors, and sizes. Yet all plants, from the fast-growing bamboo to the slow-and-steady bristlecone pine, are important regulators of earth's climate. Plants absorb carbon dioxide (CO_2) from the air through photosynthesis and thereby reduce atmospheric carbon dioxide, a **greenhouse gas** largely responsible for the rise in global temperatures associated with climate change. As plants decay and die, they contribute to the important storage of carbon in soils.

Our planet was formed about 4 billion years ago, but it was not until a couple of billion years later that free oxygen (O_2), created by microscopic organisms, began to build up in the atmosphere. Conditions slowly developed that supported more oxygen-dependent life-forms. When plants evolved, they added much more oxygen to the atmosphere. Eventually there was enough oxygen to sustain human life on earth.

According to fossil records, the first flowering plants evolved about 140 million years ago. The nectar that flowering plants produce became a food source for insects. The budding relationship between plants and insects proved mutually beneficial since insects spread

A bee in search of nectar approaching a flower.

Tortoiseshell butterflies gather on aster blossoms.

pollen (which contains a plant's genetic material) when they move from plant to plant. This process, called pollination, enabled flowering plants to reproduce much more efficiently, and they spread rapidly across the continents. Winged insects eventually evolved, and their wings made them better able to travel from plant to plant to both feed and pollinate. Along with the spread of flowering plants, insects—in sheer numbers alone—have become the most successful group of organisms on our planet today.

Insects continued to evolve alongside plants as pollinators, adapting themselves to access specific flower structures and becoming almost essential in the process. The plants responded with a rich supply of nectar and nutrients that nourished the insects. Plants and insects became tied together in a mutual bond of growth and self-preservation unlike any other on earth. In addition, with the help of their vast numbers and high reproductive rates, insects have come to be recognized as vital indicators of change, often providing the first signs of shifting climates.

Plants and their pollinators, trees, and forests serve as major players in the regulation of atmospheric carbon dioxide levels and therefore greatly influence global climate. They may also play a major role in the way our civilization adapts to the changes in climate predicted for the future.

A wide-angle view of Walden Pond.

Chapter One

Plants Rooted in a Changing World

Twenty thousand years ago, ice sheets spread like frozen deserts over large areas of North America and Eurasia. The migration of **species** that took place as the glaciers retreated has been studied by **climatologists** with the help of **ice cores** and pollen layers that hold records of Earth's vegetation. This data contains valuable historical information that is useful in predicting future changes for plants, insects, and forest covers as a result of the current human-induced climate change.

Weather is the short-term condition of the atmosphere. Weather changes daily, often many times a day. Changes occur in air temperature, brightness, cloudiness, humidity (the amount of water vapor in the air), precipitation (rain, snow, or sleet), and wind. Climate, on the other hand, is the long-term weather pattern for a given area.

There is much evidence to support the fact that climate change can affect precipitation and other weather conditions, ultimately changing the climate of an entire region. This can affect forests, **plant ranges**, insects, and entire ecosystems. During the last glacial period, for instance, plants were abundant in the equatorial region, where temperatures were more suitable. But as the ice age came to an end, over thousands of years, climates warmed and plants shifted their ranges toward the polar regions.

Small insects, plants, and free-living organisms (such as plankton and bacteria) tend to be more mobile and are therefore able to shift locations more quickly. On the other hand, larger plants such as shrubs and trees, which have evolved over thousands of years, may not be able to move or adapt fast enough to keep pace with climate change. Some plants and insects may respond to climate change by slowly moving toward cooler environments, while others may be unable to move through the modern landscape for a number of reasons: pathways may be blocked by urban development or agriculture, pollinator timing may have shifted, land may not be available, or plants may have reached the limit of their altitudinal range. Any one of these reasons could result in extinction if a plant species is unable to tolerate the changes in its **habitat**.

FYNBOS: NO PLACE TO GO

In Cape Town, South Africa, and the surrounding area, there is a unique natural vegetation of shrubs called fynbos. This region is one of the richest botanical habitats on Earth, with a higher level of plant diversity than a tropical rain forest. Out of 30,000 fynbos species, almost one-third are completely unique to this region, earning it designation as a World Heritage Site in 2004. However, climate change, invasive (non-native) species, and urban development are threatening the fynbos. Some species have already become extinct.

The frequency of fires in the region has increased due to global warming, and when fires occur in the spring (instead of in the late summer), the plants do not have time to produce their seeds—resulting in the loss of species. Many of the fynbos plants are very localized in their distribution; therefore, if they go extinct, they will be lost forever. A recent study estimates that fynbos abundance will decrease more than 60 percent by the year 2050. Fauna and Flora International, an organization that works to promote biodiversity worldwide, purchased Flower Valley, a renowned area of fynbos at the southernmost tip of South Africa. This may save the area from being overtaken by human development or invasive trees, but it will not prevent the impacts of climate change. As temperatures keep rising, many of the fynbos species will not be able to survive, and they will have nowhere to go.

According to some studies, global warming is pushing plants to change their ranges at a rate ten times greater than that recorded since the last glacial retreat.

Ecosystems consist of a delicate balance of plants, animals, insects, and the physical environment. The study of the timing of life-cycle events in living organisms in relation to climate is known as phenology. Two of the most important and well-documented effects of climate change are the early flowering of plants and the disruption of food chains. Important life-cycle events in plants, animals, and insects—such as seed dispersal in plants and migration in animals—are often intricately connected, with one event triggering another. When the timing of these events changes, the balance within an ecosystem can be thrown off. For example, a particular plant is pollinated by a specific type of butterfly. Warmer weather may be causing the plant to flower earlier in the spring, but the butterfly pollinator, which responds to different climate cues, has not yet emerged from its cocoon and is unable to pollinate its host flower. Both species may suffer; the butterfly won't have enough food, and the plants won't be pollinated.

As the **biodiversity** of an ecosystem is reduced, the strength of the ecosystem decreases. In the butterfly example above, in a highly diverse ecosystem there is a greater likelihood that another species of butterfly, or another insect entirely, will be available to pollinate the flowering plant even if the traditional pollinator is not available. The butterfly may find another food source to replace the nectar of the flowering plant that it no longer pollinates. Greater diversity, in other words, means greater ability to adapt to change. Some species will benefit from climate change, while others will be harmed;

but climate change threatens to tear at the delicate ecosystem fabric, weakening the role that certain species play—and possibly pushing them closer to extinction. This leaves the whole ecosystem weakened and vulnerable to future change.

Spring Creep

Spring creep—the early arrival, from year to year, of spring events such as flowering in plants and nesting in birds—has put some species out of balance with their ecosystems. Plants that are unable to change their flowering times to coincide with an earlier spring are decreasing in abundance.

Scientists have been able to study spring creep through an unusual method: the writings of Henry David Thoreau, a well-known nineteenth-century American philosopher and conservationist. Thoreau's 1854 *Walden*, which details the plant life around Walden Pond in Concord, Massachusetts, has proven to be a valuable reference for today's botanists studying the same ecosystems under the influence of climate change.

The average temperature in the region of Walden Pond has risen 4.3 degrees Fahrenheit (2.4 °Celsius) according to a Harvard University study. The researchers report that 27 percent of the plants that Thoreau meticulously recorded are now locally extinct. Another 36 percent are so rare that they are in danger of extinction in the near future. Some of the hardest-hit species are the lilies, orchids, violets, roses, and dogwood trees of the Walden Pond area.

Many of Thoreau's plants now flower as much as three weeks earlier than they did in the 1840s. Other, less adaptive plants have experienced sharp declines or even local extinction. The study of the Walden Pond area showed that nonnative species fared much better than the native plants, as did damaging invasive species.

How Will Higher Greenhouse Gas Levels Affect Plant Life?

Scientists have long known that carbon dioxide in the atmosphere increases temperatures on Earth. Today we call this the greenhouse effect, but it was actually first called the carbon dioxide theory when British physicist John Tyndall came up with the idea in 1861. Less well known, however, are the long-term effects that higher atmospheric levels of carbon dioxide have on plant life.

Studies show that higher carbon dioxide levels in the atmosphere can result in growth spurts in plants and trees, since carbon dioxide is an important component in the photosynthetic process. This phenomenon is known as the carbon dioxide fertilization effect; the higher carbon dioxide levels literally fertilize plants, resulting in an increase in growth.

However, recent studies show that much of the additional carbon dioxide goes into the production of fine roots and twigs rather than new wood, and any limiting resource, such as available water or nitrogen in the soil, severely affects the benefits of the additional carbon dioxide. For instance, if water is scarce, the benefits of the additional carbon dioxide may be insignificant.

The greatest increase in growth spurred by higher carbon dioxide levels is found in young forests that are on fertile soils with plenty of water to

Carbon Dioxide and the Very Hungry Caterpillar

About 56 million years ago, Earth experienced a global-warming event that created conditions similar to our current state of climate change. **Paleobotanists** studying fossilized leaves from before and after the global-warming event were able to gather information about the effects of carbon dioxide on plant growth. The scientists recorded the types and number of insect chew marks on the fossilized leaves: holes chewed by large-mouthed insects, small bumps from wasps depositing eggs, tracks of tiny bites by the larvae of moths and flies, and punctures from aphids and mites. The data showed a big jump in the percentage of leaves exhibiting damage during the warm period.

Scientists believe that the increase in carbon dioxide associated with the warming event made photosynthesis easier for plants—an example of the carbon dioxide fertilization effect in action. However, it appears that this effect resulted in increased plant growth but with no additional protein in the extra leaves. Lab studies verify this phenomenon with plants under high-carbon-dioxide conditions. The ancient insects therefore had to eat more leaves to get the same amount of nutrition they were getting from leaves grown under lower-carbon-dioxide conditions. In other words, the insects only appeared hungrier.

THE FACE OF TECHNOLOGY

At the University of Illinois scientists are studying the effects of increased concentrations of carbon dioxide and ozone gases on soybean crops—right in the field.

Free Air Concentration Enrichment (FACE) is a new technology that uses rings of pipes equipped with high-pressure gas jets that release carbon dioxide and ozone gases into the wind as it flows across the crops. The gases in the air are monitored through sensors. Without this regulation it would be impossible to determine how much gas was reaching the crops. Downwind, outside of the rings, the concentration of gases reaches background (normal) levels within 300 feet (91 meters).

With the FACE technology, entire crops can be subjected to the atmospheric gas conditions that climatologists expect by the year 2050. At the same time, the crops are exposed to natural sunlight, humidity, insect pollinators, and other natural elements.

Significantly, the FACE experiments have shown that maize, rice, soybeans, and wheat—the world's most widely used food crops—reached only half the productivity increases from higher carbon dioxide levels. The rise in ozone caused the crop yields to crash.

sustain the growth. For the United States, these re-sults indicate that future forest productivity is likely to increase in the East and decrease in the West, where water is becoming scarcer due to climate change.

Ozone (O_3), another greenhouse gas, has also increased by as much as 6 percent per decade since 1980. According to a Royal Society study in the United Kingdom, ozone levels are likely to increase by at least 50 percent by 2020. The ozone layer in the upper atmosphere prevents harmful ultraviolet (UV) light from reaching Earth; but in the lower atmosphere, ozone gas is an air pollutant that harms the respiratory systems of people and animals and damages natural ecosystems. Increases in ozone levels near the ground can reduce agricultural yields by interfering with photosynthesis and stunting the growth of some plant species.

High carbon dioxide levels may increase the growth of certain plants and fungi that contribute to the woes of asthma sufferers. Studies show a fourfold increase in those afflicted with asthma in the United States between 1980 and 2000.

Invasive Species

Invasive species are quickly becoming one of the biggest threats to ecosystem health and biodiversity around the world. Due to their adaptability to a wide range of conditions, invasive species are opportunists that can quickly enter new habitats, and take advantage of weakened or damaged ecosystems.

Climate change is providing invasive species with opportunities to extend their ranges. For example, rising temperatures lead to drier environments, causing an increase in the forest area damaged by widespread forest fires. Invasive species are able to enter the damaged areas quickly, before native species reestablish themselves.

The Japanese beetle illustrates this link between climate change and invasive species. Introduced into the United States in 1916, the Japanese beetle has been expanding its range (and its appetite) ever since. The beetle is attracted to soybean leaves, particularly those high in sugar, as a result of increasing carbon dioxide levels in the atmosphere. As temperatures and carbon dioxide levels rise, this little destroyer is eating its way to the top of the invasive species charts.

Ecological Mismatches

The plants, insects, and animals within an ecosystem are interwoven, so the response of one species to climate change is intricately connected with that of other species. For instance, there may be a mismatch in location if a butterfly expands its range in response to rising temperatures but the plant on which it lays its eggs does not adjust its range. Mismatches in timing can occur if a plant species flowers earlier in the spring but the insect that pollinates it still takes the same amount of time to develop. The flower may have passed through its pollen stage by the time the pollinator is available.

In addition to mismatches within ecosystems, the various developmental stages in the life of an insect, such as egg, nymph (or larva), pupa, and adult, may each have a different response to climate change, further complicating the prediction of climate change impacts on ecosystems.

Wetlands

Wetlands are areas where water saturates, or covers, the soil for the entire year or only during certain periods. Peat swamps, shallow lakes, marshes, mangrove forests, and floodplains are all considered types of wetlands, covering about 6 percent of earth's land area. Rising temperatures, however, are changing the flow of rivers and watersheds, causing many wetlands to dry out.

Wetlands are enormously rich in plant and tree species such as water lilies, bulrushes, cattails, sedges, cypress, black spruce, and mangroves. These diverse ecosystems harbor migratory birds, fish, a variety of amphibians and reptiles, and an assortment of aquatic and grass-loving insects. Wetlands perform valuable ecosystem services, buffering the land against storms and floods, as well as providing food and water, stabilizing shorelines, and filtering water. The conservation of wetlands is vital to combat the impacts of climate change.

Peatlands

Peatlands, composed of 90 percent water and 10 percent dead plant matter, are important wetland areas and huge **carbon sinks**. Combined, they contain more carbon than the world's rain forests. They are found in almost every country in the world and cover more than 3 percent of the world's total land area, with the largest areas found in the northern tundra regions of Canada, Russia, and northern Europe.

TIME TO ACT fact!

Carbon dioxide and nitrous oxide emissions can be greatly reduced by the restoration of drained peatlands through rehydration.

Mangrove Forests

Mangroves live in the world between the land and the sea. These highly specialized trees have salt-filtering roots and salt-excreting leaves that allow them to live in the salt water where other plants cannot survive. Mangrove forests are under threat from coastal development, shrimp-farming operations, and sea-level rise.

Mangroves are high in biodiversity and serve as nursery grounds for many fish species. They are important protective buffer zones against storm and tidal wave damage, and they stabilize soil, preventing coastal erosion. They could prove to be an important asset in stabilizing and buffering coastlines as sea levels continue to rise in this century. Mangroves also absorb carbon dioxide and store carbon in their sediments, thus reducing the impacts of rising greenhouse gas levels.

Plants with Altitude

The rise in global temperatures is affecting the range distributions of many plants, pushing some species toward cooler, higher-elevation habitats. A study of plant cover changes between 1977 and 2007 in the Santa Rosa Mountains of California found that the average elevation of the dominant plant species rose by more than 200 feet (60 m). This shift appears to be the result of an increase in the variability of precipitation, a decrease in snowfall, and warming surface temperatures—all due to changes in the regional climate.

Mountain plants, trees, and wildflowers are particularly at risk to rising temperatures since they have no escape route. As some species shift to higher altitudes, the native species face new competition for resources, including sunlight, water, and pollinators. Furthermore, as plants creep up the mountainside looking for cooler habitats, they eventually reach the top. Then there is nowhere else left to go except into extinction.

Snow in alpine regions has been melting earlier in the season due to the earlier arrival of spring. Ironically, this can lead to an increase in frost damage for mountain wildflowers. As the plants form buds and prepare to

An alpine meadow in Glacier National Park, Montana.

flower earlier, the cold night air early in the year can often bring frost, which can damage the delicate flower structures. Frost events have increased in the last decade, and flower bud damage has led to lower seed production in some species. Insects, such as fruit flies, that eat the seeds are in turn affected by the low seed supply, as are the grasshoppers that feed on the flower petals and the wasps that prey on the fruit flies.

Climate change is proceeding at an unprecedented rate that is faster than plants and insects are able to adapt to through the usual evolutionary process of genetic modification and natural selection. Some species may be able to migrate, but if their habitat is in an area to which migration is impossible, the risk of extinction doubles. Some scientists predict that if greenhouse gas emissions are not cut down, three out of every five species will be extinct by the year 2100.

A fig wasp approaching a developing fig fruit.

Chapter Two

Plants and Their Pollinators

The flowering plants and the insects that pollinate them have been an enormous success story in the evolution of planet Earth. Plants have developed specialized reproductive structures (anthers and stigma), colored petals, and intoxicating fragrances to attract pollinators. The insects in turn have evolved specialized tongues and other mouth and body parts to access the sweet flower nectar and to carry pollen from one flower to another.

Plants, like all living organisms, reproduce. The transfer of pollen is essential for the reproduction of about 90 percent of the seed-producing plant species in the world. In order to make seeds, pollen must be transferred from the male anthers of a flower to the female stigma of the same species. This transfer of pollen is performed by a variety of pollinators, including wind, insects, birds, and other animals.

Insects are by far the largest group of pollinators, pollinating two out of every three flowering plants. In many cases, plants and their insect pollinators rely on one another for survival. Neither can exist without the other; if one should go extinct, the other would likely follow within a generation or two. For instance, tiny fig wasps and fig plants have been evolving side by side for thousands of years. Today, nine hundred species of fig plants, each with its own unique wasp pollinator, are a testament to the success of this coevolution. It is these close relationships that make climate change so menacing.

Pollination is an essential ecological function because all of the seed plants in the world need to be pollinated. The loss of pollinators would be devastating not only for ecosystems, but also for the world's food supply. Close to 80 percent of the 1,400 plants that are cultivated as food crops around the world require pollination by insects and animals. An abundance of pollinators results in fruit with more flavor and higher crop yields. The value of this service for the United States alone has been estimated at $10 billion, and about $3 trillion annually on a global scale.

There are two general types of pollen: wind-borne pollen, which is light, dry, and abundant; and insect- or animal-borne pollen, which is sticky, heavy, and produced in much smaller quantities. By studying sediment layers at the bottom of ponds, lakes, and oceans, palynologists (scientists who study living and fossilized pollen) are able to determine what kinds of plants were growing at the time the sediments were deposited. Researchers used just this kind of data to conclude that flowering plants and pollen shapes evolved alongside insect pollinators for the past 100 million years. It was the early insect pollinators that helped to spread flowering plants far and wide, pollinating them and playing a key role in plant evolution.

Despite the importance of pollinators, their distribution is poorly documented. Human-induced climate change could become the most severe threat to pollinators that humanity has ever seen.

Noninsect Pollinators

The habitats of many noninsect pollinators are vulnerable to climate change. Bats are nocturnal (nighttime) pollinators, visiting night-flowering plants such as the fragrant saguaro cactus. Hummingbirds, with their slender pointed bills, pollinate colorful tubular flowers with deep nectar treasures.

Not all pollinators need to take flight to do an effective job. The long-nosed honey possum drinks nectar from the banksia flower, pollinating it in the process, while black-and-white ruffed lemurs of Madagascar pollinate the traveler's tree. On one island in New Zealand, a large gecko (a type of lizard) transfers pollen among the flax flowers. All of these noninsect pollinators are subject to the pressures that climate change is putting on their habitats, and as their survival is threatened, so is their ability to pollinate their host flowers.

The Moth's Tongue and the Star Orchids of Madagascar

In 1862, when Charles Darwin received a package from a distinguished horticulturist containing star orchids from Madagascar, he couldn't help but be astounded by the presence of their foot-long nectar spurs. He is reported to have proclaimed, "[W]ith a nectary a foot long—Good heavens what insect can suck it?" He went on to speculate that there must be a moth with a long tongue capable of accessing the nectar at the bottom of the orchid's spurs and that this might very well be the pollinator of the flower.

At the time, **entomologists** were very skeptical, and several ridiculed his theory. Forty-one years later, Darwin was proven right. A hawk moth was discovered in Madagascar with the longest tongue of any moth or butterfly in the world, reaching up to 15 inches (38 centimeters) long. This insect had coevolved with star orchids.

Observations have proven that the giant hawk moth hovers like a hummingbird in front of the orchid and then, with its long, whiplike tongue, probes deep into the flower to find its nectar (right). In the process it picks up pollen on its head and wings, later depositing the pollen on another flower as it continues to feed. Through this unique relationship the orchid is pollinated and the insect is fed.

Many such plant-pollinator relationships are vulnerable to the effects of climate change. If this particular hawk moth is no longer present at the orchid's pollination time, the plant, unable to reproduce, could become extinct in just one generation.

Spruce trees that have fallen victim to the devastating effects of the spruce bark beetle.

Chapter Three

Forests Feeling the Heat

It is important to keep our forests healthy, because they absorb one-quarter of human carbon dioxide emissions and store 45 percent of the carbon held on land. For this reason, forests are generally considered carbon sinks: they absorb carbon and thereby lessen the effects of global warming. Forests that are increasing in size or density increase the amount of carbon that they can hold.

As trees in the forest decay, some of the carbon they store is released back into the air. In most cases the amount of carbon released is less than the amount absorbed. But if the emission of carbon exceeds the amount absorbed, the forest becomes a **carbon source**, which can harm the environment. Higher temperatures are having a noticeable impact on the world's forests. Longer growing seasons, the frequency and severity of forest fires, and a shift in the range of insect pests and tree diseases are all affecting the ability of forests to regulate climate by absorbing carbon dioxide from the atmosphere.

Tropical Forests

Tropical rain forests absorb moisture out of low-lying clouds like sponges sucking water from a leaky ceiling. Their vast acreage and rich diversity make them appear relatively unaffected by the impacts of climate change, but this is definitely not the case.

Rain forests all over the world are changing. In fact, the ancient tropical forests of Queensland, Australia, renamed in 2007 the Gondwana Rainforests of Australia, are among the most endangered mountaintop forests in the world. Once covering most of Australia and Antarctica (when they were a single continent known as Gondwana) some 15 million years ago, these ancient forests rise from the waters of the Great Barrier Reef.

The Gondwana Rainforests are home to some of Australia's most diverse plants and animals, many of them **endemic species**. Seventeen species of plants are thought to have gone extinct in this region in the second half of the twentieth century. Warmer temperatures are threatening to dry out the curtain of clouds draping the mountaintops, with potentially disastrous consequences for the highly adapted endemic plant and animal species.

Boreal Forests

Boreal forests (also known as taiga) are **biomes** in the northern latitudes that are characterized by cone-bearing plants such as pine and spruce trees, called conifers. These forests account for about one-third of earth's forests and cover 5.5 million square miles (14 million square km), which is approximately 17 percent of the world's land surface. Boreal forests are major carbon sinks, exerting an enormous influence on earth's atmosphere, global climates, and the water cycle. However, they are at great risk to the temperature increases associated with climate change.

Climate change is expected to cause changes in rainfall and humidity, causing the soil in some regions to become drier. Climatologists anticipate an overall decrease in the area of boreal forests, particularly on the southern border. As the planet warms, the southern deciduous forests are expected to outcompete the conifers of the boreal forest, and scientists fear that much of the boreal forests could be lost. There is evidence to indicate that this loss is already occurring.

Forest Pests and Diseases

Insect pests, when they proliferate and reach epidemic proportions, can cause great devastation to forests. Rising temperatures are causing drier forests, which are more likely to be weakened by insect attacks. The mountain pine beetle of western Canada has spread its range and destructivity

Fire, Fire Everywhere

Wildfires destroy acres of forest. Such destructive fires can weaken forest ecosystems, reducing their biodiversity and leaving them vulnerable to invasive species, forest pests, and disease. Studies show that climate change is accelerating the intensity and frequency of forest fires.

The summer of 2010 was the hottest on record in the past 130 years in western Russia. Consistent 100 °F (40 °C) temperatures and the lack of rain created conditions that led to a surge in wildfires, which destroyed large areas of land and injured many people.

Dry conditions have also led to record-breaking wildfire destruction across the United States in the first decade of this century. Though the overall number of fires per year has been decreasing, the individual fires have been larger, resulting in a significant increase in the total area burned since the 1980s. Climatologists and **foresters** worry that this may be just a small preview of what our forests will have to deal with in a warming world.

due to warmer, drier conditions, killing millions of lodgepole pine trees. Drought-ridden forests in the American Southwest suffered bark beetle infestations that killed an estimated 20 million ponderosa pines and 50 million piñon (pinyon) pines in 2002 and 2003.

Every year in the United States, insects and pathogens (agents or germs that cause disease) infect a forested area forty-five times larger than the area damaged by fire, severely impacting the economy. Climate change is expected to negatively impact tree and ecosystem health, widening the doorway for the entry of insect pests and disease-causing pathogens.

A mountain pine beetle.

An overwintering insect, buried in the forest floor.

Chapter Four

Impact on Insects

Never underestimate a bug!

Though small in individual stature, insects are arguably the most successful life-forms on the planet. Entomologists have named close to a million species of insects throughout the world, but some think that there could be ten times as many undiscovered species.

Insects are six-legged, cold-blooded organisms. Unlike warm-blooded animals, insects have no way of regulating their internal thermostats. The temperature in their bodies is the same as that of their environment, making insects particularly vulnerable to the rising temperatures associated with climate change.

Since insects are so important for delivering ecosystem services, from pollination to plant decomposition and soil regeneration, the loss of insect species can be a severe blow to ecosystems. Some species that are less mobile than others can become trapped in habitats that have become too warm, making the insects very vulnerable to extinction. In addition, the effects of climate change can be different on each of the life-cycle stages of insects (eggs, larvae, pupae, and adults), further complicating the overall impact on insect populations.

Climate is also a very important factor in the ability of insects to overwinter (survive the cold season) in their habitat. This ability determines the number of generations a species can produce in a year, as well as their relative abundance. The impact of climate change on insect species in the cold months depends a lot on the behavior patterns of a species. For instance, some insects overwinter near the soil surface, and the snow acts as insulation. If the snow cover is reduced due to warmer, drier winters, these insects might not survive the winter. Alternatively, insect pests that have traditionally had their life cycles broken by harsh, cold winters may now survive and proliferate into even larger populations over the next season, potentially overwhelming other species.

Warmer temperatures could result in some insects moving into regions where they could not survive before. Altered wind patterns due to climate change might also affect the long-distance movement of some species. Since many insects are transmitters of disease-causing organisms for plants, animals, and humans, subtle changes in climate can affect the spread and frequency of these diseases.

Tropical insects may be among the first species to become extinct as a result of global warming. Beetles, butterflies, and other insects that live in the steamy tropics can tolerate only a narrow range of temperatures. A rise of just a few degrees can be disastrous for some tropical insects already at the limit of their temperature range. Many researchers believe that the effect of temperature on insects is by far the greatest environmental factor determining their range and survival.

Butterflies

Butterflies may seem to be wisps in the wind, but besides providing poetic inspiration, they also serve as early indicators of environmental change. Studies show that butterflies around the world are gradually moving toward the poles, fluttering their way to cooler habitats. The most comprehensive study to date tracked thirty-five nonmigratory species of European butterflies. Sixty-three percent of the species have shifted their distribution to the north by 22 to 150 miles (35 to 240 km) during the twentieth century. In contrast, only 3 percent shifted to the south.

In the eastern part of the Canadian province of Ontario, butterflies have been the object of close study for a century, with some significant changes noted in the last decade. Species never seen before are appearing on the landscape, and populations of formerly rare species have increased. The giant swallowtail, one of the showiest butterflies in Ontario, has been spotted farther and farther north through the early part of this century.

Edith's checkerspot butterfly.

Some local populations of butterflies, such as the Edith's checkerspot, have disappeared from their southern range as they shift northward and higher in altitude. A study has shown that 40 percent of the populations below 7,800 feet (2,400 m) have gone extinct. In Europe, more than 70 percent of butterfly species are in decline, and several are no longer found at all in Britain. Most species will be unable to keep up with the rate of climate change expected in the coming decades.

It is likely that more butterfly populations will be shifting northward in North America—if they haven't already—as they have in Europe. Some butterflies will not be able to move north if their habitat or the plants that they need to survive are unable to move with them.

Dragonflies

After surviving 300 million years of evolution, dragonflies around the world are in trouble due to rising temperatures and shortages of freshwater. Dragonflies spend a good part of their lives underwater during their larval stage. A dragonfly starts as an egg and then hatches into a larval form that lives either on the water's surface or near the water's edge on the surface of a plant. The larva is totally dependent on water and even breathes through gills. Dragonfly larvae often eat mosquito larvae, helping to control the mosquito population.

One-fifth of Mediterranean dragonflies and related damselflies are threatened with extinction at the regional level due to an increasing scarcity of freshwater. Most of these species are not protected, despite their high risk of extinction. Four species are already listed as extinct in the Mediterranean region. Climate change is expected to make matters worse for the dragonflies by causing even lower levels of precipitation and possible drought.

Spotted darter dragonfly feeding on nectar.

Tundra, melting in the warmer Arctic climate.

Chapter Five

Soil, Sand, and the Not-So-Frozen Tundra

Any discussion of plants in a changing climate must take into consideration the ground upon which they grow: the soil. There are thousands of different types of soil in the world, with more than 20,000 varieties in the United States alone. Each type is influenced by the underlying rock, regional climate, terrain, vegetation, and actions of human beings, particularly agriculture.

Soil is a large carbon sink, directly absorbing the carbon contained in decaying plants. Microbes and insects in the soil then accumulate additional carbon by breaking down other organisms such as animals and insects. Soils hold approximately twice as much carbon as the atmosphere does and three times the amount contained in plants. It's not hard to see why soils are considered to be so important in the carbon cycle and, consequently, in the regulation of global climate.

Carbon that is broken down in the soil is released into the atmosphere as carbon dioxide gas. Rising temperatures speed up the release of carbon dioxide, adding to atmospheric levels of the gas and consequently to global warming. To make matters worse, soils can also release methane and nitrous oxide, two other harmful greenhouse gases. An additional 0.1 percent of carbon emitted from European soils is equivalent to the carbon emission of 100 million extra cars on the road. The estimated annual loss of carbon from the soils of the United Kingdom alone exceeds 14 million tons.

The physical structure of soil can be damaged by changing temperature and rainfall patterns associated with climate change. The soil stability affects the nutrient balance, the water retention, and the population of soil organisms. Insects aid plant growth by breaking down organic matter, releasing nutrients from the soil, and creating air and waterways in the soil. As soil structure deteriorates and the diversity of organisms decreases, the types and amount of vegetation that soils can support are reduced. Damage to soil structure may also result in an increase in the vulnerability of the soil to erosion, a major problem affecting soils all over the world. Properly managed soils can absorb large quantities of carbon from the atmosphere and can yield nutrient-rich crops. Other ecosystem services that healthy soils provide are improved air quality and water quality, pollutant filtering, dust reduction, and drought resistance.

Traditional methods of agriculture use crop rotation to control insect pests, weeds, and diseases. Modern agriculture often relies more on pesticides, which may put our global food security at risk. Crop monoculture (growing the same crop year after year) depends on chemical pesticides and a steady supply of new, often genetically modified seed varieties, leaving these agricultural ecosystems very vulnerable to change. Pest and disease outbreaks could become more common as soils deteriorate and, along with the impact of climate change on crop pollinators, could threaten the productivity of our agricultural systems and our ability to feed the world's ever-growing population.

Deserts

Nearly one-third of Earth's land surface is desert. Warmer temperatures and less rainfall due to climate change threaten to upset the delicate balance of desert life. Climate change is the leading cause of desertification (the process by which land becomes desert)—one of the most serious environmental challenges of today.

Climate change is expected to drastically alter rainfall and temperature patterns along the edges of deserts and in desert mountain areas. A study conducted between 1976 and 2000 showed temperature increases in nine out of the twelve deserts studied. Droughts have increased in intensity in recent years and are projected to become even worse in the future. The rate of desert biodiversity loss is expected to double in the coming decades. A 2006 study by the United Nations Environment Programme (UNEP) indicates that more deserts are likely to become drier and larger as glaciers melt and rivers run dry.

Sand formations in a high-altitude desert of Tibet.

The Tundra: No Longer Frozen in Time

The Arctic tundra is a region found north of the boreal forest, where the ground is permafrost (permanently frozen soil). No trees grow there at all, only small shrubs, mosses, and lichens. Temperatures in the Arctic are increasing at double the global average rate. Historically, the tundra has been a storage place for much of the world's soil carbon, but now climatologists are grappling with an important question: is the tundra still absorbing carbon dioxide, or is it now a source of carbon dioxide?

Studies over the past thirty-five years suggest that the tundra is shifting from being a carbon sink to being a carbon source. Two of the reasons for this shift appear to be a lower water table and drier conditions that have changed the plant composition of the tundra area. The loss of the great carbon sink in the Arctic tundra could have huge consequences for global warming.

A 2003 report by the United Nations indicated an additional problem: widespread permafrost degradation on the floors of the boreal forests. As temperatures rise, bogs on the forest floor are releasing methane, another major greenhouse gas, in increasing quantities. In addition, warmer weather is pushing the boreal forest northward into the tundra region. About 15 percent of the tundra has been lost to the advancing tree line since the 1970s.

The Northern Peat Bog Bomb

How dangerous could an uninhabited wasteland of permafrost be? According to some scientists, very dangerous. The western Siberian peat bog covers about a half million square miles (1.3 million km²), and the mosses and lichens growing on its surface typically absorb an enormous amount of carbon from the atmosphere. Estimates place the carbon content of the bogs at one-quarter of all the carbon absorbed by the earth and vegetation since the last ice age.

As temperatures rise, the bog begins to thaw into lakes devoid of oxygen, producing methane, a greenhouse gas that is much more potent than carbon dioxide. No one really knows how fast this methane will be released into the atmosphere, but many believe that the peat bogs of Siberia are a ticking time bomb that is destined to have a major impact on the climate in the twenty-first century, releasing tens if not hundreds of billions of tons of carbon back into the atmosphere.

A student assisting in a planting program.

Chapter Six

How You Can Help

Climate change is already visibly impacting plant and insect life in the United States and around the world. The choices we make now will determine the severity of its impact in the future. Experts urge immediate action to address the causes of climate change, including a reduction in fossil fuel emissions. This could slow down the rate at which habitats are warming, protecting many species from extinction.

There are many ways in which you can take action to slow climate change. Learn more about how climate change is affecting plants and insects around the world and then share your knowledge with friends, family members, and classmates. Encourage them to make simple changes in their lives that will help the environment.

Be a Smart Shopper

Whether you're shopping for food, clothes, or other items, try to keep the environment in mind.

- Look for products made from recycled materials. These items reduce the need to harvest more natural resources, which means fewer greenhouse gases are emitted.

- Purchase sustainably farmed vegetables, fruits, fish, and meats. Sustainable agriculture improves the environment, uses resources efficiently, and works with natural biological cycles. Your local farmers' market is a good place to find sustainably farmed foods.

- Check out consignment shops for inexpensive and unique clothing. Most stores sell cool vintage pieces and unworn or lightly worn clothing and accessories.

- Buy wood products that have the FSC logo. This means that they are accredited by the FSC, or Forest Stewardship Council, an organization that certifies only products whose manufacture does not endanger the world's forests.

Recycle and Reuse

Recycling reduces the need for landfills and incinerators, and it conserves natural resources. Many products we use today can be recycled, including aluminum cans, plastic containers, paper, and clear glass. Recycling items means fewer greenhouse gas emissions are produced in the harvesting and manufacturing of natural resources. Check with your town or city to find out what the recycling procedures are for your area. Many retailers and organizations offer programs to recycle cell phones, computers, and other electronics so that they don't end up in landfills.

Composting is a great way to put yard trimmings and food byproducts that normally end up in the trash, such as banana peels, to good use. Compost naturally enriches soil, reducing the need for chemical fertilizers, which can pollute the ocean. Also, the manufacture of chemical fertilizers releases greenhouse gases that contribute to climate change.

You can also help the environment and slow climate change by finding new uses for old items, such as using an empty glass bottle as a vase. This keeps items out of landfills, thus reducing greenhouse gas emissions.

Use Less Energy

Little changes in your daily life, such as using energy-efficient lightbulbs, might not seem like much, but when lots of people make these changes, the effect is significant. Carpooling or taking public transportation reduces the amount of greenhouse gases being emitted into the air. Even air-drying your clothes instead of using a dryer saves energy, which means fewer greenhouse gas emissions.

Get Involved

If you'd like to do more to combat climate change, consider joining an environmental group. Check and see if there is an environmental club at your school and, if not, ask a teacher to help you start one. You will meet classmates who are also concerned about the environment and want to work together to make a difference.

You can also look at what programs in your school promote the reduction of fossil fuel emissions. Most schools have a recycling program that includes paper, glass, aluminum, and plastic. Encourage your classmates to recycle, since all of these products can end up littering habitats. If your school has a cafeteria, look at how the food is packaged. Are the containers recyclable? If not, ask a teacher to help you find out if it's possible to use recyclable containers.

You can help prevent the extinction of a species by working with people who have a lot of experience in conservation. Join an environmental organization that helps protect plants and insects and their habitats. You can also make a difference by tracking changes in the climate through the observation of plant and insect behavior. Through the power of the Internet, citizen science is taking on a whole new life as ongoing research programs use volunteers to monitor natural resources. Here are some excellent organizations:

www.arborday.org/

www.plant-for-the-planet.org/en

http://monarchwatch.org/

Check out these websites to learn how you can join!

Every single tree makes a difference to the regulation of the climate and the atmosphere in which we live. Planting trees is one of the best ways to counteract excessive greenhouse gas emissions, to replace trees lost in wildfires, to support important insect life in the air and soil, and to beautify the environment. Insects are very important to the environment—from pollination to soil health—but they can also be harmful if a rapidly changing climate upsets the natural balances and relationships in ecosystems. The sooner we start taking action to slow climate change, the better!

Glossary

biodiversity The variation of living organisms within an ecosystem, or on the entire Earth.

biomes A large area with distinctive vegetation and animal groups adapted to that particular environement.

carbon sinks Natural or human-made carbon reservoirs that store more carbon than they release—for example, natural forests or oceans.

carbon source Any natural or human-made carbon reservoir that releases more carbon that it absorbs.

climatologists Scientists who study climates.

endemic species Species of plants or animals that are native to a specific region and live nowhere else on Earth.

entomologists Scientists who study insects.

foresters Persons who manage forests.

greenhouse gas A gas such as carbon dioxide, that prevents heat from escaping Earth's atmosphere, contributing to global warming.

habitat The natural environment in which a species lives.

ice cores Long tubes of ice extracted from glaciers and polar sea ice.

lichens Plantlike organisms consisting of a fungus and either algae or cyanobacteria (a blue-green algae) living together in a successful partnership.

paleobotanists Scientists who study the fossil records of plants.

plant ranges   The geographic locations where species naturally grow.

species   A group of organisms capable of breeding together and producing fertile offspring.

p. 10. "Some plants and insects . . . cooler environments.": Brian Huntley, "How Plants Respond to Climate Change: Migration Rates, Individualism and the Consequences for Plant Communities," *Annals of Botany* 67 (1991): 15-22.

p. 12, "According to some studies . . .": Ronald Neilson et al, "Forecasting Regional to Global Plant Migration in Response to Climate Change," *Bioscience* (2005): 55.

p. 13, "Another 36 percent . . . near future.": Charles G. Willis, "Phylogenetic Patterns of Species Loss in Thoreau's Woods Are Driven by Climate Change," *Proceedings of the National Academy of Sciences* 105, no. 44 (2008): 17029-17033.

p. 13, "Spring arrives in the United States . . .": U.S. Climate Change Science Program (CCSP), *Thresholds of Climate Change in Ecosystems.* Synthesis and Assessment Products 4.2 (Washington, DC: United States Global Change Research Program, 2009) , pp. 36-37.

p. 15, "Scientists believe . . . conditions": Evan H. DeLucia et al., "Insects Take a Bigger Bite Out of Plants in a Warmer, Higher Carbon Dioxide World," *Proceedings of the National Academy of Sciences (PNAS)* 105, no. 6 (2008): 1781-1782.

p. 17, "The greatest . . . due to climate change.", p. 38.: CCSP, 2009.

p. 17, "Increases in ozone . . .": Randall Mutters, *Statewide Potential Crop Yield Losses from Ozone Exposure* (Air Resources Board, Los Angeles: California Environmental Protection Agency, 1998), p. 29.

p. 17, "High carbon dioxide levels . . .": Lewis H. Ziska, Paul R. Epstein, and William H. Schlesinger, "Rising CO_2, Climate Change, and Public Health: Exploring the Links to Plant Biology," *Environmental Health Perspectives* 117, no. 2 (2009): 155-158.

p. 18, "The Japanese beetle . . .": Daniel A. Potter and David W. Held, "Biology and Management of the Japanese Beetle," *Annual Review of Entomology* 47 (2002): 175-205.

p. 18, "As temperatures and carbon . . .": Nicola L. Ward and Gregory J. Masters, "Linking Climate Change and Species Invasion: An Illustration Using Insect Herbivores," *Global Change Biology* 13, no. 8 (2007): 1605-1615.

p. 18, "The plants, insects, and . . .": Walther Gian-Reto, "Community and Ecosystem Responses to Recent Climate Change," *Philosophical Transactions of the Royal Society B* 365, no. 1549 (2010): 2019-2024.

p. 19, "Carbon dioxide and . . .": Couwenberg, John, "Methane Emissions from Peat Soils," Wetlands International, Ede. Produced for the UNFCCC meetings in Bonn, August 2009.

p. 21, "Insects, such as fruit . . .": David Inouye, "Warmer Springs Mean Less Snow, Fewer Flowers in the Rockies," *Ecology,* (2008).

p. 21, "Some species may . . .": Chris D. Thomas et al, "Extinction Risk from Climate Change," *Nature* 427 (2004): 145-148.

p. 22, "Pollination is . . .": U.S. Forest Service, "Celebrating Wildflowers: What Is Pollination?," www.fs.fed.us/wildflowers/pollinators/whatispollination.shtml.

p. 24, "[W]ith a nectary . . .": Charles Darwin, "Letter 3411: January 25, 1862," Darwin Correspondence Project, www.darwinproject.ac.uk/entry-3411.

p. 25, "flowering plants and pollen . . .": Shusheng Hu et al, "Early Steps of Angiosperm-Pollinator Coevolution," *PNAS* 105, no. 1 (2008): 240-245.

p. 25, "Despite the importance . . .": J. T. Kerr, "Butterfly Species Richness Patterns in Canada: Energy, Heterogeneity, and the Potential Consequences of Climate Change," *Conservation Ecology* 5, no. 1 (2001): 10.

p. 30, "Their vast acreage . . .": J. Alan Pounds, "Amphibian Declines and Climate Disturbance: The Case of the Golden Toad and the Harlequin Frog," *Conservation Biology Vol. 8, No. 1* (1994): 72-85.

p. 30, "Seventeen species . . .": "Queensland Tropical Rain Forests," World Wildlife Fund, 2001, http://worldwildlife.org/ecoregions/aa0117.

pp. 30-31, "Warmer temperatures are . . .": Stephen E. Williams, Elizabeth E. Bolitho, and Samantha Fox, "Climate Change in Australian Tropical Rainforest: An Impending Environmental Catastrophe," *Proceedings of the Royal Society B* (2003): 270.

p. 31, "These forests account . . .": Glenn P. Juday et al, "Importance and Relationship of Boreal Forests to Climate," *Encyclopedia of Earth*, May 8, 2010, updated October 16, 2012. www.eoearth.org/article/Importance_and_relationship_of_boreal_forests_to_climate.

p. 32, "Consistent 100 °F . . .": Michael Schwirtz, "Moscow Weather Back to Normal after Fires," *New York Times*, August 19, 2010, www.nytimes.com/2010/08/20/world/europe/20moscow.html?_r=1&ref=forest_and_brush_fires.

p. 33, "Drought-ridden forests . . .": David D Breshears et al, "Regional Vegetation Die-off in Response to Global-Change-Type Drought," *PNAS* 102, no. 42 (2005): 15144-15148.

p. 37, "the effect of temperature . . .": J. S. Bale et al, "Herbivory in Global Climate Change Research: Direct Effects of Rising Temperatures on Insect Herbivores," *Global Change Biology* 8 (2002): 1-16.

p. 37, "The most comprehensive . . .": Camille Parmesan et al, "Poleward Shifts in Geographical Ranges of Butterfly Species Associated with Regional Warming," *Nature* 399 (1999): 579-583.

pp. 37-38, "Species never seen . . .": Hall, *Sentinels on the Wing*, 2009, p. 6.

p. 38, "In Europe . . . in Britain": Chris D. Thomas et al, "Comparative Losses of British Butterflies, Birds, and Plants and the Global Extinction Crisis," *Science* 303, no. 5665 (2004): 1879-1881.

p. 42, "The estimated annual loss . . .": Pat H. Bellamy et al, "Carbon Losses from All Soils Across England and Wales 1978-2003," *Nature* 437 (2005): 245-248.

p. 44, "A 2006 study . . .": United Nations Environment Programme, "Global Deserts Outlook," UNEP Assessment (Nairobi: United Nations Environment Programme, 2006).

p. 44, "the tundra is shifting . . . source": Walter Oechel et al, "Recent Change of Arctic Tundra Ecosystems from a Net Carbon Dioxide Sink to a Source," *Nature* 361 (1993): 520-523.

p. 45, "About 15 percent . . .": Food and Agriculture Organization of the United Nations, *State of the World's Forests* (Geneva: Food and Agriculture Organization of the United Nations, 2003).

p. 45, "As temperatures rise . . .": L. C. Smith et al, "Siberian Peatlands a Net Carbon Sink and Global Methane Source Since the Early Holocene," *Science* 303, no. 5656 (2004): 353-356.

p. 45, "No one really knows . . .": Fred Pearce, *With Speed and Violence: Why Scientists Fear Tipping Points in Climate Change* (Boston: Beacon Press, 2007).

Bibliography

Angert, A. et al. "Drier Summers Cancel Out The Carbon Dioxide Uptake Enhancement Induced By Warmer Springs." *Proceedings of the National Academy of Sciences* 102, no. 31 (2005): 10823-10827.

Arbor Day Foundation. *Zone Changes.* 2006. http://www.arborday.org/media/mapchanges.cfm.

Bale, J. S. et al. "Herbivory in Global Climate Change Research: Direct Effects of Rising Temperatures on Insect Herbivores." *Global Change Biology* 8 (2002): 1-16.

Bellamy, Pat H. "Carbon losses from all soils across England and Wales 1978–2003." *Nature* 437 (2005): 245-248.

Breshears, David D. et al. "Regional Vegetation Die-off in Response to Global-Change-Type Drought." *Proceedings of the National Academy of Sciences* 102, no. 42 (2005): 15144-15148.

Ciais, P. et al. "Europe-wide Reduction in Primary Productivity Caused by the Heat and Drought in 2003." *Nature* 437 (2005): 529-533.

Currano, Ellen et al. "Sharply Increased Insect Herbivory During the Paleocene–Eocene Thermal Maximum." *Proceedings of the National Academy of Sciences* 105, no. 6 (2008): 1960-1964.

Darwin, Charles. "Letter 3411." Darwin Correspondence Project. January 25, 1862. http://www.darwinproject.ac.uk/entry-3411

De Lucia, Evan et al. "Insects Take a Bigger Bite Out of Plants in a Warmer, Higher Carbon Dioxide World." *Proceedings of the National Academy of Sciences* 105, no. 6 (2008): 1781-1782.

Djoghlaf, Dr. Ahmed, Executive Secretary of the Convention on Biological Diversity, interview by Message to the Media. *World Day to Combat Desertification* (June 17, 2010).

Earthwatch Institute. *Climate Change Threatens Pollination Timing.* August 9, 2006. http://www.sciencedaily.com /releases/2006/08/060809234056.htm.

Edwards, Robin, ed. Provisional Atlas of the Aculeate Hymenoptera of Britain and Ireland Parts 1–4 (1997–2001). Huntingdonshire, England: Monks Wood Experimental Station, 2001.

European Forest Fire Information System. "Forest Fires in Europe." *Welcome to EFFIS.* May 23, 2010. http://effis.jrc.ec.europa.eu/current-situation.

Food and Agriculture Organization of the United Nations. *State of the World's Forests.* Geneva: Food and Agriculture Organization of the United Nations, 2003.

Gedney, N., P. M. Cox, and C. Huntingford. "Climate Feedback From Wetland Methane Emissions." *Geophysical Research Letters* 31 (2004): L20503.

Gian-Reto, Walther. "Community And Ecosystem Responses To Recent Climate Change." *Philosophical Transactions of the Royal Society B* 365, no.1549 (2010): 2019-2024.

Hall, Peter W. *Sentinels on the Wing—The Status and Conservation of Butterflies in Canada.* Ottawa: NatureServe Canada, 2009.

Hu, Shusheng et al. "Early Steps of Angiosperm—Pollinator Coevolution." *Proceedings of the National Academy of Sciences* 105, no. 1 (2008): 240-245.

Huntley, Brian. "How Plants Respond to Climate Change: Migration Rates, Individualism and the Consequences for Plant Communities." *Annals of Botany* 67 (1991): 15-22.

Inouye, David. "Warmer Springs Mean Less Snow, Fewer Flowers in the Rockies." *Ecology*, 2008.

Intergovernmental Panel on Climate Change. *IPCC Fourth Assessment Report: Climate Change (AR4).* Assessment Report 4. Geneva: Intergovernmental Panel on Climate Change, 2007.

Kerr, J. T. "Butterfly Species Richness Patterns in Canada: Energy, Heterogeneity, and the Potential Consequences of Climate Change." *Conservation Ecology* 5, no. 1: (2001): 10.

Kurz, W. A. et al. "Mountain Pine Beetle And Forest Carbon Feedback To Climate Change." *Nature* 452 (2008): 987-990.

Lenoir, J. et al. "A Significant Upward Shift in Plant Species' Optimum Elevation during the 20th Century." *Science* (2008): 320.

Lovejoy, Thomas E., and Lee Hannah, eds. *Climate Change and Biodiversity.* New Haven, CT: Yale University Press, 2004.

Masters, Karen. "Responses of Natural Communities to Climate Change in a Highland Tropical Forest." In *Climate Change and Biodiversity*, edited by Thomas E. Lovejoy and Lee Hannah. New Haven: Yale University Press, 2005.

Millet, Bruce. "Climate Trends of the North American Prairie Pothole Region 1906–2000." *Climatic Change* (2009): 243-267.

Mutters, Randall. *Statewide Potential Crop Yield Losses from Ozone Exposure.* Air Resources Board, LA: California Environmental Protection Agency, 1998.

Neilson, Ronald et al. "Forecasting Regional to Global Plant Migration in Response to Climate Change." *Bioscience* (2005): 55.

Oechel, Walter et al. "Recent Change of Arctic Tundra Ecosystems from a Net Carbon Dioxide Sink to a Source." *Nature* 361 (1993): (6412): 520-523.

Parmesan, Camille et al. "Poleward Shifts in Geographical Ranges of Butterfly Species Associated with Regional Warming." *Nature* 399 (1999): 579-583.

Pearce, Fred. *With Speed and Violence: Why Scientists Fear Tipping Points in Climate Change.* Boston: Beacon Press, 2007.

Pitelka, Louis. "Plant Migration and Climate Change." *American Scientist* (1997): 85.

Potter, Daniel A. and David W. Held. "Biology and Management of the Japanese Beetle." *Annual Review of Entomology* 47 (2002): 175-205 .

Pounds, J. Alan. "Amphibian Declines and Climate Disturbance: The Case of the Golden Toad and the Harlequin Frog." *Conservation Biology* (1994): 72-85.

Savinar, Matt. *Facts and Research.* June 22, 2010. www.lifeaftertheoilcrash.net/Research.html.

Smith, L. C. et al. "Siberian Peatlands: A Net Carbon Sink and Global Methane Source Since the Early Holocene." *Science* 303, no. 5656 (2004): 353-356.

Thomas, Chris D. et al. "Comparative Losses of British Butterflies, Birds, and Plants and the Global Extinction Crisis." *Science* 303, no. 5665 (2004): 1879-1881.

Thuiller, Wilfred et al. "Climate Change Threats To Plant Diversity In Europe." *Proceedings of the National Academy of Sciences* 102, no. 23 (2005): 8245-8250 .

Turetsky, Merritt R. et al. "Wildfires Threaten Mercury Stocks in Northern Soils." *Geophysical Research Letters* (2006): 33.

United Nations Environment Programme. *Global Deserts Outlook.* Assessment, Nairobi: United Nations Environment Programme, 2006.

United Nations Framework Convention on Climate Change. *Methane Emissions From Peat Soils (Organic Soils, Histosols).* Bonn: United Nations Framework Convention on Climate Change, 2009.

University of Illinois at Urbana Champaign. *SoyFace.* USDA ARS. September 01, 2009. http://soyface.illinois.edu/technology.htm.

U.S. Climate Change Science Program. *Thresholds of Climate Change in Ecosystems.* Synthesis and Assessment Products 4, no. 2. Washington: United States Global Change Research Program, 2009.

Ward, Nicola L., and Gregory J. Masters. "Linking Climate Change and Species Invasion: An Illustration Using Insect Herbivores." *Global Change Biology* 13, no. 8 (2007): 1605-1615.

Williams, Stephen et al. "Climate Change in Australian Tropical Rainforest: An Impending Environmental Catastrophe." *Proceedings of the Royal Society B* (2003): 270.

Willis, Charles G. "Phylogenetic Patterns of Species Loss in Thoreau's Woods Are Driven by Climate Change." *Proceedings of the National Academy of Sciences* 105, no. 44 (2008): 17029-17033 .

World Wildlife Fund. "Queensland Tropical Rain Forests." World Wildlife Fund, 2001. www.worldwildlife.org/wildworld/profiles/terrestrial/aa/aa0117_full.html.

Index

Page numbers in **bold** are photographs, illustrations, and maps.

About the Author

Stephen Aitken is fascinated by the natural world and its remarkable diversity. He is the author of many books for young people from third grade to high school, written for publishers all over the world. Aitken is a biologist and senior editor of *Biodiversity*, a peer-reviewed science journal, and executive secretary of Biodiversity Conservancy International. He is a vegetarian, does not own a car, and tries to keep his carbon footprint as close to his shoe size as possible. The author's studio in the beautiful Himalayas of India provides shelter for ants and spiders, baby geckos, and an odd orange-eared mouse.

For a complete list of books that Aitken has written and illustrated, please visit www.stephenaitken.com.